WHY DO THE SEASONS CHANGE?

MELISSA STEWART

Marshall Cavendish
Benchmark
New York

Marshall Cavendish Benchmark
99 White Plains Road
Tarrytown, New York 10591-9001
www.marshallcavendish.us

Editor: D. Sanders
Editorial Director: Michelle Bisson
Art Director: Anahid Hamparian
Series Designer: Alex Ferrari

Library of Congress Cataloging-in-Publication Data

Stewart, Melissa.
Why do the seasons change? / by Melissa Stewart.
p. cm. — (Tell me why, tell me how)
Summary: "An examination of the phenomena and scientific principles behind
the changing of the seasons"—Provided by publisher.
Includes bibliographical references and index.
ISBN-13: 978-0-7614-2112-2 (alk. paper)
ISBN-10: 0-7614-2112-2 (alk. paper)
1. Seasons—Juvenile literature. 2. Earth—Rotation—Juvenile literature.
3. Earth—Orbit—Juvenile literature. I. Title. II. Series.

QB637.4.S74 2006
523'.5—dc22

2005017263

Photo research by Candlepants Incorporated

Cover photo: Herman Eisenbeiss/Photo Researchers Inc.

The photographs in this book are used by permission and through the courtesy of: *Corbis:* Don Mason, 1, Images.com, 4; Royalty Free, 7; Chase Swift, 8; gds/zefa, 11; NASA/JPL-Caltech, 12; Jolanda Cats & Hans Withoos/zefa, 14. *Photo Researchers Inc:* Victor Habbick Visions, 10; Mark Garlick, 15, 19, 23; Jim Zipp, 24 (both), 25 (both); Richard Hutchings, 26. *SuperStock:* Mike Robinson, 5, 6; age fotostock, 18.

Printed in Malaysia
1 3 5 6 4 2

CONTENTS

An artist shows what the
four seasons might look like
for the same tree.

The Four Seasons

Earth is our home planet. It is made up of seven **continents,** or large areas of land, and a lot of water. North America is a continent made up of three large countries—Canada, the United States, and Mexico.

In North America, the weather changes during the year. Winter is the coldest **season.** In many places snow falls, and

In most of North America, winter snow makes for hours of fun.

lakes and ponds freeze. When people go outside, they often wear coats, mittens, and hats to stay warm.

In spring and summer, people like to spend more time outside.

In spring the air warms up, and the ground begins to thaw. Plants sprout or start to grow new leaves. Many birds return from their warmer winter homes. They build nests and lay eggs. Spring is a time of new life.

In summer the days are long and hot. Plants grow, and flowers bloom. Animals raise their young. Summer is a time for being outdoors—running, swimming, and having fun with your friends.

In some parts of North America, autumn is a colorful time of year. The

Autumn arrives in a burst of color.

Each autumn, geese and many other birds fly south.

leaves of many trees turn orange, red, or yellow. Then the leaves fall to the ground.

The cool days of autumn tell animals it is time to get ready for the winter ahead. Some birds and insects begin a long journey to warmer places. Other animals grow a thick, warm coat and curl up in a cozy **burrow.** Still others gather food to eat during the long, cold winter ahead.

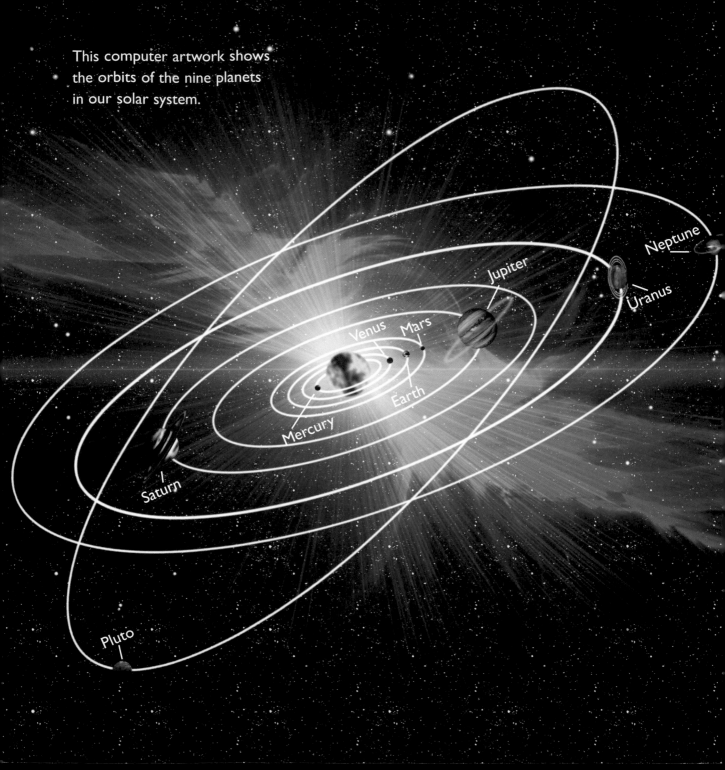

This computer artwork shows the orbits of the nine planets in our solar system.

Neptune

Uranus

Jupiter

Venus Mars

Earth

Mercury

Saturn

Pluto

Moving Around the Sun

Earth seems huge to us, but it is just one of nine planets in our **solar system.** The other planets are Mercury, Venus, Mars, Jupiter, Saturn, Uranus, Neptune, and Pluto.

All the planets **orbit,** or move around, the Sun. The Sun is a star. It gives off the heat and light that make life on Earth possible.

It takes Earth about 365 days—or one Earth **year**—to make a full orbit. This

Earth orbits the Sun, drawing in some of the Sun's heat and light.

11

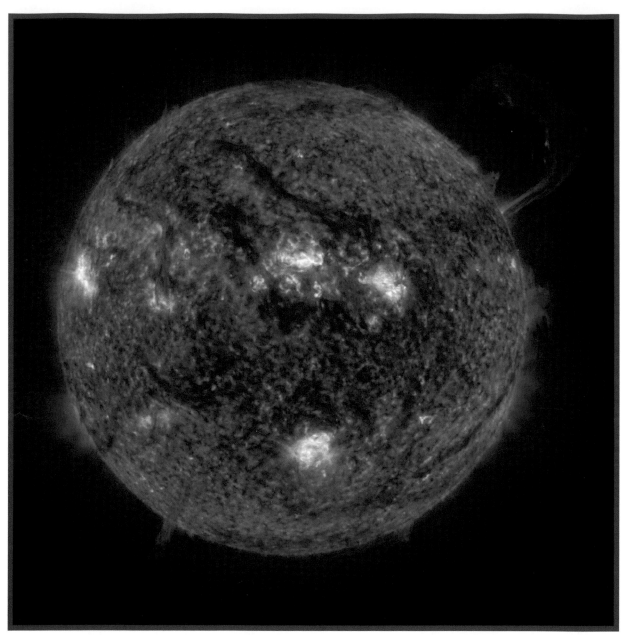

The Sun plays a major role in Earth's changing seasons.

means that between your last birthday and your next birthday, Earth will make one complete trip around the Sun.

Now I Know!

What two planets are closer to the Sun than Earth is?

Mercury and Venus.

Mercury and Venus are closer to the Sun. They orbit the Sun more quickly than Earth does. So they have shorter years.

Mars, Jupiter, Saturn, Uranus, Neptune, and Pluto are farther from the Sun. It takes longer for them to travel around the Sun. So they have longer years. Pluto is so far from the Sun that a year on Pluto is 247 times longer than a year on Earth.

In the middle of the day, the Sun is high in the sky. Never look directly at the Sun. It could harm your eyes.

Spinning Round and Round

Earth orbits the Sun. It also spins, like a top, at the same time. As Earth spins, different parts of the planet face the Sun. It is daytime in the places that are facing the Sun. That is why days are usually bright and sunny. It is nighttime on the part of Earth that is turned away from the Sun. That is why it is dark at night. It takes about twenty-four hours—or one full day—for Earth to spin completely around once.

To see this for yourself, remove the shade from a lamp. Then

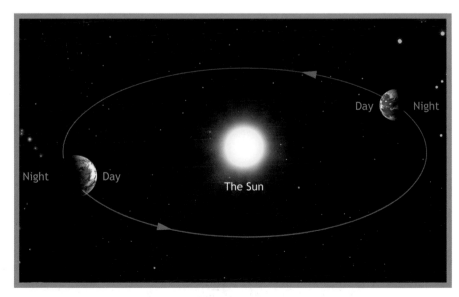

Day   Night

Night   Day

The Sun

It is always daytime on the part of Earth that is facing the Sun.

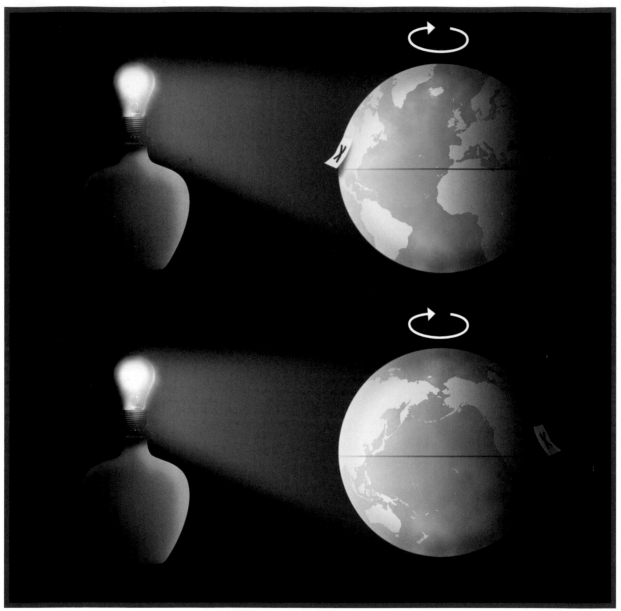

In the activity, daytime is when the place you live is facing the lightbulb. When your hometown is in shadow, then it is night.

place a **globe** near the lightbulb. Pretend the lightbulb is the Sun.

On the globe, mark the place where you live with a small piece of paper with an X on it. Turn on the lamp, and turn off all the other lights in the room. Then slowly spin the globe. When light falls on the piece of paper, it is daytime where you live. When the piece of paper crosses into shadow, night begins. Night continues until the piece of paper is lit up again.

During the summer, the Sun shines directly on the place where you live. The days are long and can be quite hot.

☀ A Tilted Earth ☀

Like a lollipop on a stick, Earth spins around an imaginary line that runs through the center of the planet between the North Pole and the South Pole. This imaginary line is called the **axis.**

If you look closely at a globe, you will see that Earth's axis is tilted, or tipped, a little bit. That is why North America gets more hours of daylight in the summer than in the winter.

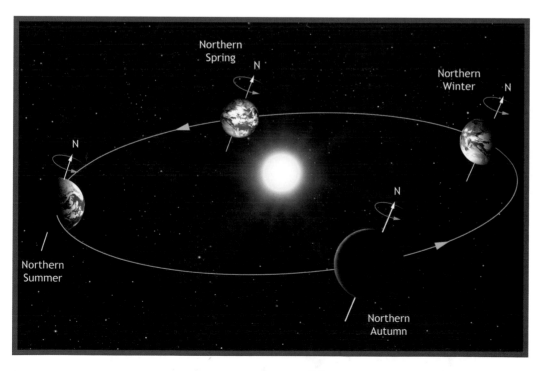

This computer artwork shows the position of the Sun during each season.

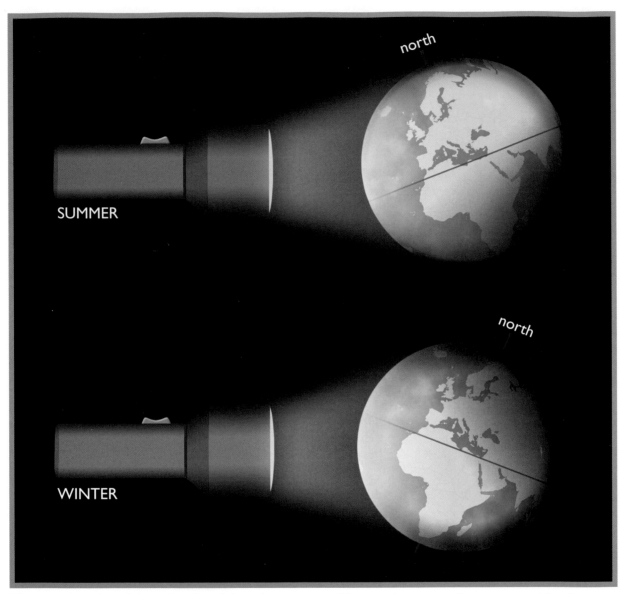

The top drawing shows the tilt of the planet around June—the start of summer in North America (which is facing the flashlight). The bottom drawing shows the planet in December—a time of cold and little daylight in North America.

To see this for yourself, stand about 3 feet (0.9 meter) from a globe. Have a friend tip the globe toward you. Turn off all the lights in the room and shine a flashlight on the place where you live. This is what happens in the summer for people who live in North America. The Sun shines directly on the area where you live. The days are long and hot.

Keep holding the flashlight in the same position. Ask a friend to tip the globe away from you. This is what happens in the winter. The Sun shines directly on the lower half of the world. The top part gets less of the Sun's light and thus less of its warmth. In North America, winter days are short and cold.

On this globe, North America is shown on top. South America is pictured below. The equator runs through its upper part.

Why Do the Seasons Change?

Take another look at the globe. Notice that the continents of North America, Europe, part of Africa, and most of Asia are above, or north, of the **equator**, the imaginary line around the middle of Earth. The part of the world above the equator

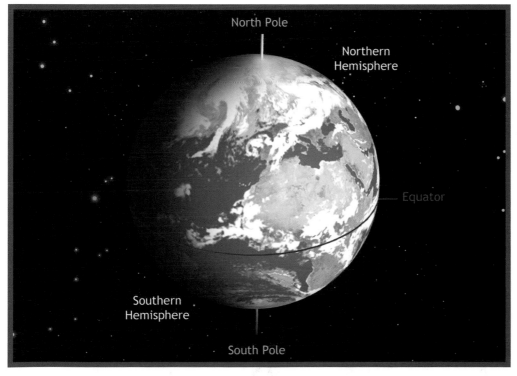

North Pole

Northern Hemisphere

Equator

Southern Hemisphere

South Pole

This computer artwork of Earth shows the position of the equator.

is called the Northern Hemisphere. The part of the world below the equator is called the Southern Hemisphere.

When the North Pole is tipped closest to the Sun, it is summer for people living in the Northern Hemisphere. The air, ground, and water warm up as the Sun's rays shine directly on the oceans and land.

A tour of the seasons: spring . . .

summer . . .

24

When the North Pole is tipped farthest from the Sun, it is winter for people living in the Northern Hemisphere. The Sun's rays are much weaker, so the air, ground, and water cool down. In many places, ice forms on lakes and ponds, and snow falls from the sky.

During spring and autumn, Earth is tipped only a little.

autumn . . .   and winter.

In autumn, the air grows cooler. Days and nights are more equal in length. It can be a great time to play outdoors.

The number of hours in a day and the number of hours in a night are about the same. But as time passes and our world continues to orbit the Sun, Earth's tilt slowly changes and our planet soon slips into a new season.

Now I Know!

What is the name of the imaginary line that divides Earth in half?

The equator.

 Activity

During the summer, the Sun shines directly on the place where you live. To show that the summer sun really heats the things it shines on, try this experiment. You will need a bowl, aluminum foil, a stick that is shorter than the bowl's width, a marshmallow, plastic wrap, and a rubber band.

1. Line the inside of a bowl with aluminum foil. Fold down any parts that stick over the edge.
2. Find a thin stick that is a little shorter than the bowl's width. Slide a marshmallow onto the stick and place it in the bowl.
3. Cover the bowl with plastic wrap. Use a rubber band to hold it in place.
4. Put the bowl in a sunny spot, and check it every fifteen minutes. How long does it take for the marshmallow to feel warm and soft?
5. Repeat the experiment at other times of the year. What happens then?

 Glossary

axis—An imaginary line that runs between a planet's north pole and south pole.

burrow—A hole in the ground where an animal sleeps or rests.

continent—A large area of land that is often surrounded by water. Earth has seven continents. They are North America, South America, Asia, Europe, Africa, Australia, and Antarctica.

equator—An imaginary line running around the middle of a planet that divides it in half.

globe—A model of Earth.

orbit—The path a planet follows as it moves around the Sun.

season—Our planet's tilt affects the amount of daylight hours a place on Earth receives during specific periods of the year. When it is summer where you live, the part of Earth you live on is tipped toward the Sun. Direct sunlight makes the days long and hot. In winter your home is tipped away from the Sun. The days are short and cold.

solar system—The region of space surrounding a particular star. Our solar system surrounds the Sun.

year—The amount of time it takes for a planet to travel once around the Sun.

 Find Out More

BOOKS

Arnosky, Jim. *Crinkleroot's Nature Almanac*. New York: Simon & Schuster Books, 1999.

dePaola, Tomie. *Four Stories for Four Seasons*. New York: Aladdin, 1994.

Gibbons, Gail. *The Reason for the Seasons*. New York: Holiday House, 1996.

Ruiz, Andres Llamas. *Seasons*. New York: Sterling, 1997.

VanCleave, Janice. *Janice VanCleave's Science around the Year*. New York: John Wiley, 2000.

WEB SITES

The Seasons and Axis Tilt
http://www.enchantedlearning.com/subjects/astronomy/planets/earth/Seasons.shtml
View a diagram that explains what causes Earth's seasons.

Winter Weatherlore and Folklore Forecasts
http://www.stormfax.com/wxlore.htm
This site features fun ideas about the relationship between summer and winter weather. It will give you a good laugh.

 Index

Page numbers for illustrations are in **boldface.**